Easy blooms from the desert or the flower garden fly off your needles for never-wilting, floral flourishes. Add felted covers to coordinate mismatched pots or vases and plant hangers to make hanging gardens.

LEISURE ARTS, INC.
Maumelle, Arkansas

CACTUS PINCUSHION

●●○○ EASY

Approximate Finished Size: 5½" tall x 2½" wide (14 cm x 6.5 cm) excluding pot

Shopping List

Yarn (Medium Weight) MEDIUM 4

[3.5 ounces, 186 yards
(100 grams, 170 meters) per ball]:

- ☐ Green - 1 ball
- ☐ Yellow - 20 yards (18.5 meters)

Knitting Needles

Double pointed, set of 5

- ☐ Size 5 (3.75 mm)
  or size needed for gauge

Additional Supplies

- ☐ Split ring marker
- ☐ Yarn needle
- ☐ Polyester fiberfill
- ☐ 2½" (6.5 cm) tall clay pot
- ☐ Hot glue gun and glue sticks

Gauge Information

Gauge is not of great importance; your pieces may be a little larger or smaller without changing the overall effect.

Techniques Used

- Knit increase ***(Figs. 4a & b, page 41)***
- Knit purl increase ***(Fig. 6, page 42)***
- K2 tog ***(Fig. 8, page 42)***
- P2 tog ***(Fig. 15, page 45)***

Cactus

With Green, cast on 12 sts. Divide sts onto 4 double pointed needles; place marker to indicate beginning of rnd ***(see Markers, page 39 and Circular Knitting, page 40)***.

Rnd 1 (Right side)**:** Knit around.

Rnd 2: Knit increase around: 24 sts.

Rnd 3: ★ Knit purl increase, K1, P1; repeat from ★ around: 32 sts.

Rnd 4: (P1, K1) around.

Rnd 5: (K1, P1) around.

Rnds 6-31: Repeat Rnds 4 and 5, 13 times.

Rnd 32: ★ K2 tog, (P1, K1) twice, P2 tog; repeat from ★ 2 times **more**: 24 sts.

Cut yarn leaving a long end for sewing.

Thread yarn needle with long end and slip sts from needles onto yarn; draw sts up tightly and secure end.

Stuff Cactus firmly with polyester fiberfill.

Sew cast on edge closed.

Flower

With Yellow, cast on 16 sts. Divide sts onto 4 double pointed needle; place marker to indicate beginning of rnd.

Rnd 1 (Right side)**:** (K1, P1) around.

Rnd 2: (P1, K1) around.

Rnds 3-8: Repeat Rnds 1 and 2, 3 times.

Cut yarn leaving a long end for sewing.

Thread yarn needle with long end and slip sts from needles onto yarn; draw sts up tightly and secure end.

Stuff Flower with polyester fiberfill.

Sew cast on edge closed; do **not** cut yarn. Sew Flower to top of Cactus with same end; secure end.

Use hot glue gun to secure bottom of Cactus in clay pot.

COASTERS

EASY

Approximate Finished Size: 4½" (11.5 cm) diameter (from Petal to Petal)

Shopping List

Yarn (Medium Weight) MEDIUM 4

[3.5 ounces, 186 yards
(100 grams, 170 meters) per ball]:

- ☐ Yellow - 1 ball
- ☐ Brown - 1 ball
- ☐ Gold - 1 ball

Knitting Needles

Straight,

- ☐ Size 6 (4 mm)

Additional Supplies

- ☐ Stitch markers

Gauge Information

Gauge is not of great importance; your pieces may be a little larger or smaller without changing the overall effect.

Techniques Used

• K3 tog *(Fig. 9, page 43)*

Flower

Center (Make 3 **each** with Brown and Gold)

With color indicated, cast on 7 sts.

Row 1 (Right side)**:** P1, (K, P, K) **all** in next st, P1, K1, P1, (K, P, K) **all** in next st, P1: 11 sts.

Rows 2-4: P1, (K1, P1) across.

Row 5: P1, (K, P, K) **all** in next st, P1, (K1, P1) across to last 2 sts, (K, P, K) **all** in next st, P1: 15 sts.

Rows 6-16: P1, (K1, P1) across.

Row 17: P1, K3 tog, P1, (K1, P1) across to last 4 sts, K3 tog, P1: 11 sts.

Rows 18-20: P1, (K1, P1) across.

Row 21: P1, K3 tog, P1, (K1, P1) across to last 4 sts, K3 tog, P1: 7 sts.

Bind off all sts in pattern.

Petals

Place 8 markers evenly spaced around Center.

First Petal

With **right** side facing and Yellow, pick up 5 sts across Center across to first marker *(Figs. 16a & b, page 45)*.

Row 1: Knit across.

Row 2: K2, **turn**; slip 1 as if to **knit**, K1.

Row 3: K3, **turn**; slip 1 as if to **knit**, K2.

Row 4: K4, **turn**; slip 1 as if to **knit**, K3.

Row 5: K3, **turn**; slip 1 as if to **knit**, K2.

Row 6: K2, **turn**; slip 1 as if to **knit**, K1.

Bind off 4 sts in **knit**: one st remaining on right needle.

Next 7 Petals

Pick up 4 sts across to next marker: 5 sts.

Work same as First Petal: one st remaining on right needle.

At end of last Petal, pick up one st at base of First Petal, pass second st over first st and off needle, cut yarn and pull yarn through last st.

SACHET BAG

EASY

SACHET BAG

Finished Size: 6½" wide x 7½" high (16.5 cm x 19 cm)

Shopping List

Yarn (Fine Weight)

[3.5 ounces, 317 yards
(100 grams, 290 meters) per skein]:

- ☐ Cream - 1 skein
- ☐ Purple - 30 yards (27.5 meters)
- ☐ Green - 20 yards (18.5 meters)

Knitting Needles

Straight,

- ☐ Size 4 (3.5 mm) **or** size needed for gauge
- ☐ Size 3 (3.25 mm)

Additional Supplies

- ☐ Tapestry needle
- ☐ Sewing needle and matching thread
- ☐ Crochet hook, size G (for stem)
- ☐ ¼" (6 mm) wide ribbon - 24" (61 cm) length

Gauge Information

With larger size needles, in Stockinette Stitch (knit one row, purl one row), 23 sts and 29 rows = 4" (10 cm)

Techniques Used

- Adding new sts ***(Figs. 3a & b, page 41)***
- Knit increase ***(Figs. 4a & b, page 41)***
- YO ***(Fig. 7, page 42)***
- K2 tog ***(Fig. 8, page 42)***
- Slip 1, K1, PSSO ***(Figs. 10a & b, page 43)***
- Slip 1, K2 tog, PSSO ***(Fig. 11, page 43)***

Body (Make 2)

With Cream and using larger size needles, cast on 38 sts.

Row 1 (Right side)**:** Knit across.

Row 2: Purl across.

Row 3: K1, ★ K2 tog, K2, YO, K1, YO, K2, slip 1, K1, PSSO; repeat from ★ across to last st, K1.

Row 4: Purl across.

Row 5: K2, ★ K2 tog, YO, K3, YO, slip 1, K1, PSSO, K2; repeat from ★ across.

Row 6: Purl across.

Rows 7-42: Repeat Rows 1-6, 6 times.

Rows 43-46: Beginning with a **knit** row, work in Stockinette St.

Row 47 (Eyelet row)**:** K2, ★ YO, K2 tog, K2; repeat from ★ across.

Row 48: Purl across.

Rows 49-52: Repeat Rows 43-46.

Rows 53 and 54: Knit across.

Bind off all sts in **knit**.

Sew bottom and side seams.

Flower (Make 3)

With Purple and using smaller size needles, place slip knot on needle: one st.

Row 1: Knit increase: 2 sts.

Row 2: Purl across.

Row 3: Knit increase, K1: 3 sts.

Row 4: Purl across.

Row 5: K2, add on 3 sts; bind off 3 sts: 3 sts.

Row 6: Purl across.

Rows 7-12: Repeat Rows 5 and 6, 3 times.

Row 13: Slip 1, K2 tog, PSSO: one st.

Cut Purple.

Place last st on crochet hook; with Green, ch 12 for stem ***(see Crochet Stitches, page 46)***; finish off.

Using photo as a guide for placement, sew Flowers to Bag.

Weave ribbon through Eyelet Row and tie ends in a bow.

MUG COZY

●●○○ **EASY**

Finished Size: 3" wide x 11" long (7.5 cm x 28 cm)

Shopping List

Yarn (Medium Weight) MEDIUM 4

[3.5 ounces, 186 yards (100 grams, 170 meters) per ball]:

- ☐ Green - 1 ball
- ☐ Yellow - 1 ball
- ☐ Ecru - 1 ball

Knitting Needles

Straight,

- ☐ Size 5 (3.75 mm) **or** size needed for gauge

Additional Supplies

- ☐ Sewing needle and matching thread
- ☐ 7/16" (11 mm) buttons - 4

Gauge Information

In pattern, 15 sts = 3" (7.5 cm)

Techniques Used

- Adding new sts ***(Figs. 3a & b, page 41)***
- YO ***(Fig. 7, page 42)***
- K2 tog ***(Fig. 8, page 42)***
- P2 tog ***(Fig. 15, page 45)***

Stitch Guide

BOBBLE (uses one st)
(K, P, K, P, K) **all** in same st, **turn**; K5, **turn**; P5, **turn**; K5, **turn**; P2 tog twice, P1; with yarn in **back**, pass second and third st on right needle over first st.

Cozy

With Green, cast on 7 sts.

Rows 1 and 2: K1, (P1, K1) across.

Row 3 (Buttonhole row)**:** K1, P1, K1, YO, K2 tog, P1, K1.

Rows 4-10: K1, (P1, K1) across.

Row 11: Add on 4 sts, K1, (P1, K1) across: 11 sts.

Row 12: Add on 4 sts, K1, (P1, K1) across: 15 sts.

Repeat Row 1 for pattern until piece measures approximately 11" (28 cm) from cast on edge.

Bind off all sts in pattern.

Flower

(Make 2 with Yellow and one with Ecru)

With color indicated, cast on 4 sts.

Row 1 (Wrong side)**:** Knit across.

Row 2: Work Bobble, P2, **turn**; slip 1 as if to **knit**, K2: 4 sts.

Row 3: Purl across.

Rows 4-12: Repeat Rows 1-3, 3 times.

Row 13: Knit across.

Row 14: Work Bobble, bind off all sts in **purl** leaving a long end for sewing.

Using long end, sew first and last Petals together.

Using photo as a guide for placement, sew Flowers to Cozy. Sew a button to the Center of each Flower and to opposite end of Cozy from buttonhole.

CACTUS GARDEN & HANGER

●●○○ EASY

CACTUS GARDEN

Approximate Finished Size: 7½" tall x 8" wide (19 cm x 20.5 cm) (including bowl)

Shopping List

Yarn

(Medium Weight) MEDIUM 4
[3.5 ounces, 170 yards (100 grams, 156 meters) per skein]:

- ☐ Grey - 1 skein
- ☐ Sage - 1 skein
- ☐ Dk Green - 1 skein
- ☐ Green - 1 skein
- ☐ Teal - 1 skein
- ☐ Pink - 1 skein

(Super Bulky) SUPER BULKY 6
[1.75 ounces, 27 yards (50 grams, 25 meters) per skein]:

- ☐ Off White - 10 yards (9 meters)

Knitting Needles

Double pointed, set of 5

- ☐ Size 9 (5.5 mm)

Circular, 16" (40.5 cm) length

- ☐ Size 9 (5.5 mm)

Additional Supplies

- ☐ Split ring marker
- ☐ Yarn needle
- ☐ Glass bowl - 3" high x 6½" opening (7.5 cm x 16.5 cm)
- ☐ Round floral foam - 1 $^{3}/_{16}$" thick x 5 $^{7}/_{8}$" diameter (3 cm x 15 cm)
- ☐ Polyester fiberfill
- ☐ Straight pins
- ☐ Moss - optional

Gauge Information

Gauge is not of great importance; your pieces may be a little larger or smaller without changing the overall effect.

Techniques Used

- tbl *(Fig. 2, page 41)*
- Knit increase *(Figs. 4a & b, page 41)*
- Knit purl increase *(Fig. 6, page 42)*
- K2 tog *(Fig. 8, page 42)*

Soil

With Grey, cast on 12 sts. Divide sts onto 4 double pointed needles; place marker to indicate beginning of rnd *(see Markers, page 39 and Circular Knitting, page 40)*.

Rnd 1 (Right side)**:** Knit around.

Rnd 2 AND ALL EVEN NUMBERED RNDS: Purl around.

Rnd 3: (K2, knit increase) around: 16 sts.

Rnd 5: (K1, knit increase) around: 24 sts.

Rnd 7: (K2, knit increase) around: 32 sts.

Rnd 9: (K3, knit increase) around: 40 sts.

Rnd 11: (K4, knit increase) around: 48 sts.

Rnd 13: (K5, knit increase) around: 56 sts.

Rnd 15: (K6, knit increase) around: 64 sts.

Rnd 17: (K7, knit increase) around: 72 sts.

Rnd 19: (K8, knit increase) around: 80 sts.

Rnd 21: (K9, knit increase) around: 88 sts.

Rnd 23: (K 10, knit increase) around: 96 sts.

Rnd 25: (K 11, knit increase) around: 104 sts.

Bind off all sts in **purl**.

Thin Cactus (Make 3)

With Sage, cast on 9 sts. Divide sts onto 3 double pointed needles; place marker to indicate beginning of rnd.

Rnd 1 (Right side)**:** Knit around.

Rnd 2: Purl around.

Repeat Rnds 1 and 2 until piece measures 2½" (6.5 cm) from cast on edge for short Cactus; 3½" (9 cm) for medium Cactus; and 4½" (11.5 cm) for tall Cactus.

Cut yarn leaving a long end for sewing.

Thread yarn needle with long end and slip sts from needles onto yarn; draw sts up tightly and secure end.

Stuff Cactus with polyester fiberfill.

Sew cast on edge closed.

Barrel Cactus

With Dk Green, cast on 16 sts. Divide sts onto 4 double pointed needles; place marker to indicate beginning of rnd.

Rnd 1 (Right side)**:** Knit around.

Rnd 2: Knit increase around: 32 sts.

Rnds 3-15: K1 tbl, P2, (K2 tbl, P2) around to last st, K1 tbl.

Cut yarn leaving a long end for sewing.

Thread yarn needle with long end and slip sts from needles onto yarn; draw sts up tightly and secure end.

Stuff Cactus with polyester fiberfill.

Sew cast on edge closed.

Using photo as a guide for placement, weave Off White yarn from bottom to top between the knit sts and secure ends.

Succulent

With Teal and using circular needle, cast on 30 sts.

Rows 1 and 2: Knit across.

Row 3: Knit increase across: 60 sts.

Rows 4-6: Knit across.

Row 7: Knit increase across: 120 sts.

Row 8: Knit across.

Cut yarn.

With Sage, bind off all sts in **knit**.

Tall Cactus

With Green, cast on 12 sts. Divide sts onto 3 double pointed needles; place marker to indicate beginning of rnd.

Rnd 1: Knit around.

Rnd 2: ★ Knit purl increase, K1, P1; repeat from ★ around: 16 sts.

Rnd 3: (P1, K1) around.

Rnd 4: (K1, P1) around.

Rnds 5-20: Repeat Rnds 3 and 4, 8 times.

Cut yarn leaving a long end for sewing.

Thread yarn needle with long end and slip sts from needles onto yarn; draw sts up tightly and secure end.

Stuff Cactus with polyester fiberfill.

Sew cast on edge closed.

Flower

With Pink, work same as Tall Cactus through Rnd 12.

Cut yarn leaving a long end for sewing.

Thread yarn needle with long end and slip sts from needles onto yarn; draw sts up tightly and secure end.

Stuff Flower with polyester fiberfill.

Sew cast on edge closed; do **not** cut yarn. Sew Flower to top of Tall Cactus with same end; secure end.

Finishing

Pin Soil to floral foam.

Using photo as a guide for placement, sew Cacti and Succulent to Soil.

Place Soil in bowl and add moss around the edges to stabilize the arrangement.

PLANT HANGER

Finished Size: 8" (20.5 cm) diameter

Shopping List

Yarn (Medium Weight) MEDIUM 4

[3.5 ounces, 170 yards (100 grams, 156 meters) per skein**]**:

☐ 1 skein

Knitting Needles

Double pointed, set of 5

☐ Size 9 (5.5 mm) **or** size needed for gauge

Additional Supplies

☐ Split ring marker

☐ Yarn needle

☐ 1½" (4 cm) metal ring

☐ Crochet hook, size G - optional

Gauge Information

In pattern, 16 sts = 4" (10 cm)

Techniques Used

- Knit increase ***(Figs. 4a & b, page 41)***
- YO ***(Fig. 7, page 42)***
- K2 tog ***(Fig. 8, page 42)***

Body

Cast on 12 sts. Divide sts onto 4 double pointed needles; place marker to indicate beginning of rnd ***(see Markers, page 39 and Circular Knitting, page 40)***.

Rnd 1 (Right side)**:** Knit around.

Rnd 2: (YO, K1) around: 24 sts.

Rnd 3: Knit around.

Rnd 4: (YO, K2 tog) around.

Rnds 5 and 6: Repeat Rnds 3 and 4.

Rnd 7: ★ K1, knit increase, K3, knit increase; repeat from ★ around: 32 sts.

Rnd 8: (YO, K2 tog) around.

Rnd 9: Knit around.

Rnd 10: (YO, K2 tog) around.

Rnd 11: ★ K1, knit increase, K5, knit increase; repeat from ★ around: 40 sts.

Rnd 12: (YO, K2 tog) around.

Rnd 13: Knit around.

Rnd 14: (YO, K2 tog) around.

Rnd 15: ★ K1, knit increase, K7, knit increase; repeat from ★ around: 48 sts.

Rnd 16: (YO, K2 tog) around.

Rnd 17: Knit around.

Rnd 18: (YO, K2 tog) around.

Rnd 19: ★ K1, knit increase, K9, knit increase; repeat from ★ around: 56 sts.

Rnd 20: (YO, K2 tog) around.

Rnd 21: Knit around.

Rnd 22: (YO, K2 tog) around.

Rnd 23: ★ K1, knit increase, K 11, knit increase; repeat from ★ around: 64 sts.

Rnd 24: (YO, K2 tog) around.

Rnd 25: Knit around.

Rnd 26: (YO, K2 tog) around.

Rnd 27: ★ K1, knit increase, K 13, knit increase; repeat from ★ around: 72 sts.

Rnd 28: (YO, K2 tog) around.

Rnd 29: Knit around.

Rnds 30 and 31: Repeat Rnds 28 and 29.

Bind off all sts in **knit**.

Hanger

Cut eight, 30" (76 cm) strands of yarn and set aside.

With **right** side of Body facing, pick up 3 sts ***(Fig. 16b, page 45)*** across bound off edge.

Row 1: K3, slide sts to opposite end of needle.

Repeat Row 1 for pattern until Hanger measures 11" (28 cm).

Cut yarn, leaving an approximately 20" (51 cm) long end.

Thread yarn needle with two lengths of set aside yarn and slip sts from needle onto yarn; tie all strands in a bow to prevent raveling.

Skipping 15 sts on cast on edge from previous Hanger, repeat for 3 more Hangers.

Optional

Using crochet hook, work single crochet around metal ring until completely covered; join with slip st to first sc, finish off ***(see Crochet Stitches, page 46)***.

Untie bows on Hanger strands; then pull all yarn ends through ring. Tie strands in an overhand knot around ring, making sure Hangers are equal in length before tightening knot.

Wrap a long strand of yarn around ends of strands below the knot until they are covered; secure ends.

Thread yarn needle with a 6" (15 cm) strand of yarn and weave through cast on sts at bottom of Body; pull tightly and secure end.

BOUQUET

●●○○ EASY

Finished Size: Approximately 8" wide x 9" high (20.5 cm x 23 cm) including pot

Shopping List

Yarn (Fine Weight) FINE 2

[3.5 ounces, 317 yards (100 grams, 290 meters) per ball**]**:

- ☐ Dk Pink - 1 ball
- ☐ Pink - 1 ball
- ☐ Cream - 1 ball
- ☐ Purple - 1 ball
- ☐ Green - 1 ball

Knitting Needles

Straight,

- ☐ Size 3 (3.25 mm)

Additional Supplies

- ☐ Tapestry needle
- ☐ 5" (12.5 cm) floral foam ball
- ☐ 4" (10 cm) tall clay pot
- ☐ 20 gauge floral wire
- ☐ Needle nose pliers
- ☐ Hot glue gun and glue sticks

Gauge Information

Gauge is not of great importance; your pieces may be a little larger or smaller without changing the overall effect.

Techniques Used

- Adding new sts ***(Figs. 3a & b, page 41)***
- Knit increase ***(Figs. 4a & b, page 41)***
- Purl increase ***(Fig. 5, page 42)***
- K2 tog ***(Fig. 8, page 42)***
- Slip 1, K2 tog, PSSO ***(Fig. 11, page 43)***
- Slip 2 tog, K1, P2SSO ***(Figs. 13a & b, page 44)***
- SSK ***(Figs. 14a-c, page 44)***
- P2 tog ***(Fig. 15, page 45)***

Rosebud

With Dk Pink, cast on 6 sts.

Row 1 (Increase row)**:** Knit increase, knit across: 7 sts.

Row 2 (Right side - Increase row)**:** Purl across to last 2 sts, purl increase, P1: 8 sts.

Rows 3 and 4: Repeat Rows 1 and 2: 10 sts.

Row 5: Knit across.

Row 6: Purl across.

Rows 7 and 8: Repeat Rows 5 and 6.

Row 9 (Decrease row)**:** K1, K2 tog, knit across: 9 sts.

Row 10 (Decrease row)**:** Purl across to last 3 sts, P2 tog, P1: 8 sts.

Rows 11-20: Repeat Rows 1-10: 10 sts.

Rows 21-24: Repeat Rows 1-4: 14 sts.

Rows 25-30: Repeat Rows 5-8 once, then repeat Rows 5 and 6 once **more**.

Rows 31 and 32: Repeat Rows 9 and 10: 12 sts.

Rows 33-36: Repeat Rows 1-4: 16 sts.

Rows 37-44: Repeat Rows 5-8 twice.

Rows 45-56: Repeat Rows 9 and 10, 6 times: 4 sts.

Row 57: K1, K2 tog, K1: 3 sts

Row 58: P2 tog, P1: 2 sts.

Row 59: K2 tog: one st.

Cut yarn and pull through last st.

With **right** side facing and beginning at cast on edge, roll Rosebud loosely. Push Center up slightly and sew through bottom of piece to secure. Roll top edges outwards.

Rosebud Leaf (Make 3)

With Green and leaving a long end for sewing, place slip knot on needle: one st.

Row 1 (Right side)**:** (K, P, K) **all** in same st: 3 sts.

Row 2: K1, P1, K1.

Row 3: Knit increase, K1, knit increase: 5 sts.

Row 4: K2, P1, K2.

Row 5: Knit increase, K3, knit increase: 7 sts.

Row 6: K3, P1, K3.

Row 7: Knit across.

Row 8: K3, P1, K3.

Rows 9 and 10: Repeat Rows 7 and 8.

Row 11: K2, slip 2, K1, P2SSO, K2: 5 sts.

Row 12: K2, P1, K2.

Row 13: K1, slip 2, K1, P2SSO, K1: 3 sts.

Row 14: K1, P1, K1.

Row 15: Slip 1, K2 tog, PSSO: one st.

Cut yarn and pull through last st.

Using beginning long end, sew each Leaf to bottom of Rosebud.

Rose (Make 6)

With Dk Pink, cast on 6 sts.

Row 1 (Increase row)**:** Knit increase, knit across: 7 sts.

Row 2 (Right side - Increase row)**:** Purl across to last 2 sts, purl increase, P1: 8 sts.

Row 3: Knit across.

Row 4: Purl across.

Row 5 (Decrease row)**:** K1, K2 tog, knit across: 7 sts.

Row 6 (Decrease row)**:** Purl across to last 3 sts, P2 tog, P1: 6 sts.

Rows 7-18: Repeat Rows 1-6 twice: 6 sts.

Rows 19-22: Repeat Rows 1 and 2 twice: 10 sts.

Rows 23-26: Repeat Rows 3 and 4 twice.

Rows 27-30: Repeat Rows 5 and 6 twice: 6 sts.

Rows 31-54: Repeat Rows 19-30 twice: 6 sts.

Rows 55-60: Repeat Rows 1 and 2, 3 times: 12 sts.

Rows 61-66: Repeat Rows 3 and 4, 3 times.

Rows 67-72: Repeat Rows 5 and 6, 3 times: 6 sts.

Rows 73-90: Repeat Rows 55-72: 6 sts.

Rows 91-93: Repeat Rows 5 and 6 once, then repeat Row 5 once **more**: 3 sts.

Row 94: P2 tog, P1: 2 sts.

Row 95: K2 tog: one st.

Cut yarn and pull through last st.

With **right** side facing and beginning at cast on edge, roll Rose loosely. Push Center up slightly and sew through bottom of piece to secure. Roll top edges outwards.

Carnation

Petals (Make 9 with Dk Pink, 6 with Pink, and 3 **each** with White and Purple)

With color indicated, cast on 6 sts.

Row 1 (Right side)**:** Purl across.

Row 2: Add on 3 sts, bind off 3 sts, knit across.

Rows 3-16: Repeat Rows 1 and 2, 7 times.

Bind off all sts in **purl**.

With **right** side facing and beginning at cast on edge, roll Carnation loosely. Sew through bottom of piece to secure.

Base (Make 21)
With Green, cast on 5 sts.

Row 1 (Right side)**:** Purl across.

Row 2: Add on one st, bind off one st, knit across.

Rows 3-14: Repeat Rows 1 and 2, 6 times.

Bind off all sts in **purl**, leaving a long end for sewing.

With **right** sides facing, sew a Base around bottom of a Carnation.

Carnation Leaf
(Make 63)

With Green, cast on 3 sts.

Row 1 (Right side)**:** Knit increase, K1, knit increase: 5 sts.

Row 2: K2, P1, K2.

Row 3: Knit across.

Row 4: K2, P1, K2.

Rows 5-12: Repeat Rows 3 and 4, 4 times.

Row 13: SSK, K1, K2 tog: 3 sts.

Row 14: Slip 1, K2 tog, PSSO: one st.

Cut yarn leaving a long end for sewing and pull through last st.

Sew cast on edges of 3 Leaves to each Carnation Base.

Finishing
Glue foam ball to clay pot.

Cut floral wire into 28, 4-5" (10-12.5 cm) long pieces.

Push a wire from bottom to top through Center of each Flower. Using needle nose pliers, bend top tip of wire into a hook shape. Pull wire hook back into Center of Flower.

Push Rosebud wire into foam ball at top Center. Alternate 3 Roses with 3 Carnations around Center Rosebud. Attach remaining 3 Roses under Carnations. Attach remaining Carnations to foam ball, arranging Leaves and Flowers to cover ball.

FELTED BOWL & VASE

●●○○ EASY

Approximate Finished Size:

Bowl - 2¼" high x 3½" diameter (5.75 cm x 9 cm)

Vase - 4" high x 3" diameter (10 cm x 7.5 cm)

Shopping List

Yarn (Medium Weight) MEDIUM 4

100% Wool

[1.75 ounces, 109 yards

(50 grams, 99 meters) per skein]:

☐ 1 skein will make both

Knitting Needles

Double pointed, set of 5

☐ Size 8 (5 mm)

Gauge Information

Gauge is not of great importance; your pieces may be a little larger or smaller without changing the overall effect.

Techniques Used

- Knit increase *(Figs. 4a & b, page 41)*
- K2 tog *(Fig. 8, page 42)*

Bowl

Cast on 12 sts. Divide sts onto 4 double pointed needles; place marker to indicate beginning of rnd ***(see Markers, page 39 and Circular Knitting, page 40).***

Rnd 1 (Right side)**:** Knit around.

Rnd 2: K1, knit increase, (K2, knit increase) around to last st, K1: 16 sts.

Rnd 3: Knit around.

Rnd 4: (K1, knit increase) around: 24 sts.

Rnd 5: Knit around.

Rnd 6: (K2, knit increase) around: 32 sts.

Rnds 7 and 8: Knit around.

Rnd 9: (K3, knit increase) around: 40 sts.

Rnds 10 and 11: Knit around.

Rnd 12: (K4, knit increase) around: 48 sts.

Rnds 13 and 14: Knit around.

Rnd 15: (K5, knit increase) around: 56 sts.

Rnds 16 and 17: Knit around.

Rnd 18: (K6, knit increase) around: 64 sts.

Rnds 19-24: Knit around.

Rnd 25: (K6, K2 tog) around: 56 sts.

Rnds 26 and 27: Knit around.

Rnd 28: (K5, K2 tog) around: 48 sts.

Rnds 29 and 30: Knit around.

Bind off all sts in **knit**.

Vase

Work same as Bowl through Rnd 15: 56 sts.

Rnds 16-44: Knit around.

Rnd 45: (K5, K2 tog) around: 48 sts.

Rnds 46 and 47: Knit around.

Rnd 48: (K4, K2 tog) around: 40 sts.

Rnds 49 and 50: Knit around.

Bind off all sts in **knit**.

Felting

Secure all ends and clip close to piece.

Felt Vase and Bowl in separate lingerie bags or pillowcases tied at the top.

Set washer for the hottest water setting possible with a cold rinse cycle. Add a very small amount of detergent. Agitation is an important factor to felting; place an **old** pair of jeans in the washer to help speed up the process.

Do **not** allow the washer to go to the spin cycle. Check every few minutes during the wash cycle to keep an eye on size and shrinkage to see if the felting is complete. Once the stitches become hard to see and the size of pieces are approximately the desired finished size, remove them from the machine and allow the wash water to spin out. Place the pieces back in for a cold rinse. Roll the pieces separately in clean towels and gently squeeze out the excess water. Do not wring the towels as that may set in permanent creases. Shape the pieces and place something heavy inside each to flatten the bottom; allow to dry completely.

TABLE RUNNER

EASY

Finished Size: 11" wide x 50" long (28 cm x 127 cm)

Shopping List

Yarn (Medium Weight) 4 MEDIUM

[3.5 ounces, 170 yards
(100 grams, 156 meters) per skein]:

Runner:

☐ Taupe - 3 skeins

[3.5 ounces, 186 yards
(100 grams, 170 meters) per skein]:

Roses and Leaves:

☐ Dk Pink - 1 skein
☐ Wine - 1 skein
☐ Pink - 1 skein
☐ Green - 1 skein
☐ Yellow - 1 skein

Knitting Needles

Straight,

☐ Size 10 (6 mm) **and**
☐ Size 7 (4.5 mm)
or sizes needed for gauge

Double pointed,

☐ Size 7 (4.5 mm) (for Stem only)

Additional Supplies

☐ Sewing needle and matching thread

Gauge Information

In Runner pattern, 18 sts = 4" (10 cm)

Techniques Used

- Adding new sts ***(Figs. 3a & b, page 41)***
- Knit increase ***(Figs. 4a & b, page 41)***
- Purl increase ***(Fig. 5, page 42)***
- Knit purl increase ***(Fig. 6, page 42)***
- YO ***(Fig. 7, page 42)***
- K2 tog ***(Fig. 8, page 42)***
- Slip 1, K1, PSSO ***(Figs. 10a & b, page 43)***
- Slip 1, K2 tog, PSSO ***(Fig. 11, page 43)***
- Slip 1, K2, PSSO ***(Fig. 12, page 44)***
- P2 tog ***(Fig. 15, page 45)***

Runner

With Taupe and using larger size needles, cast on 51 sts.

Rows 1-6: K1, (P1, K1) across.

Row 7 (Right side)**:** (K1, P1) twice, K2, ★ YO, slip 1, K2, PSSO; repeat from ★ across to last 6 sts, K2 tog, (P1, K1) twice: 50 sts.

Row 8 AND ALL WRONG SIDE ROWS: K1, (P1, K1) twice, purl across to last 5 sts, K1, (P1, K1) twice.

Row 9: (K1, P1) twice, K2, ★ slip 1, K2, PSSO, YO; repeat from ★ across to last 5 sts, K1, (P1, K1) twice.

Row 11: (K1, P1) twice, K2, ★ YO, slip 1, K2, PSSO; repeat from ★ across to last 5 sts, K1, (P1, K1) twice:

Repeat Rows 8-11 for pattern until piece measures approximately 48" (122 cm) from cast on edge, ending by working Row 8.

Next Row: (K1, P1) across to last 6 sts, knit purl increase, K1, (P1, K1) twice: 51 sts.

Last 5 Rows: K1, (P1, K1) across.

Bind off all sts in pattern.

Rosebud (Make 3 with Dk Pink and 2 with Wine)

With color indicated and using smaller size needles, cast on 4 sts.

Row 1 (Increase row)**:** Knit increase, K3: 5 sts.

Row 2 (Right side - Increase row)**:** Purl across to last 2 sts, purl increase, P1: 6 sts.

Rows 3 and 4: Repeat Rows 1 and 2: 8 sts.

Row 5: Knit across.

Row 6: Purl across.

Rows 7 and 8: Repeat Rows 5 and 6.

Row 9: K1, K2 tog, knit across: 7 sts.

Row 10: Purl across to last 3 sts, P2 tog, P1: 6 sts.

Row 11: Knit across.

Row 12: Purl across.

Row 13 (Increase row)**:** Knit increase, knit across: 7 sts.

Row 14 (Increase row)**:** Purl across to last 2 sts, purl increase, P1: 8 sts.

Rows 15 and 16: Repeat Rows 13 and 14: 10 sts.

Row 17-22: Repeat Rows 11 and 12, 3 times.

Row 23 (Decrease row)**:** K1, K2 tog, knit across: 9 sts.

Row 24 (Decrease row)**:** Purl across to last 3 sts, P2 tog, P1: 8 sts.

Row 25: Knit across.

Row 26: Purl across.

Rows 27-50: Repeat Rows 13-26 once, then repeat Rows 13-22 once **more**: 10 sts.

Row 51 (Decrease row)**:** K1, K2 tog, knit across: 13 sts.

Row 52 (Decrease row)**:** Purl across to last 3 sts, P2 tog, P1: 12 sts.

Rows 53-61: Repeat Rows 51 and 52, 4 times; then repeat Row 51 once **more**: 3 sts.

Row 62: P2 tog, P1: 2 sts.

Row 63: K2 tog: one st.

Cut yarn and pull through last st.

With **right** side facing and beginning at cast on edge, roll Rosebud loosely. Push Center up slightly and sew through bottom of piece to secure. Roll top edges outward.

Base (Make 4)

With Green and using smaller size needles, cast on 4 sts.

Row 1: Purl across.

Row 2 (Right side)**:** Add on 3 sts, bind off 3 sts, K3: 4 sts.

Row 3: Purl across.

Row 4: Knit across.

Rows 5-20: Repeat Rows 1-4, 4 times.

Bind off all sts in **purl**.

Stem

With **right** side facing, using smaller size needles, and Green, pick up 12 sts evenly spaced across ends of rows along straight edge of Base *(Fig. 16a, page 45)*.

Row 1: Purl across.

Row 2 (Decrease row)**:** K2 tog across: 6 sts.

Rows 3 and 4: Repeat Rows 1 and 2: 3 sts.

Slip sts onto one double pointed needle and work I-cord as follows:

Row 1: K3, slip sts to opposite end of double pointed needle.

Repeat Row 1 until I-cord measures approximately 4½-5" (11.5-12.5 cm).

Bind off all sts in **knit**.

Rose (Make 3 **each** with Wine, Dk Pink, Pink, and Yellow)

With color indicated and using smaller size needles, cast on 4 sts.

Row 1 (Increase row)**:** Knit increase, K3: 5 sts.

Row 2 (Right side - Increase row)**:** Purl across to last 2 sts, purl increase, P1: 6 sts.

Row 3: Knit across.

Row 4: Purl across.

Row 5 (Decrease row)**:** K1, K2 tog, knit across: 5 sts.

Row 6 (Decrease row)**:** Purl across to last 3 sts, P2 tog, P1: 4 sts.

Rows 7-24: Repeat Rows 1-6, 3 times.

Rows 25-28: Repeat Rows 1 and 2 twice: 8 sts.

Rows 29-32: Repeat Rows 3 and 4 twice.

Rows 33-36: Repeat Rows 5 and 6 twice: 4 sts.

Rows 37-48: Repeat Rows 25-36.

Rows 49-54: Repeat Rows 1 and 2, 3 times: 10 sts.

Rows 55-60: Repeat Rows 3 and 4, 3 times.

Rows 61-66: Repeat Rows 5 and 6, 3 times: 4 sts.

Rows 67-84: Repeat Rows 49-66.

Row 85: K1, K2 tog, K1: 3 sts.

Row 86: P1, P2 tog: 2 sts.

Row 87: K2 tog: one st.

Cut yarn and pull through last st.

With **right** side facing and beginning at cast on edge, roll up Rose loosely. Push Center up slightly and sew through bottom of piece to secure. Roll top edges outward.

Small Leaf (Make 20)

With Green and using smaller size needles, place slip knot on needle: one st.

Row 1 (Right side)**:** (K, P, K) **all** in same st: 3 sts.

Row 2: K1, P1, K1.

Row 3: Knit increase, K1, knit increase: 5 sts.

Row 4: K2, P1, K2.

Row 5: Knit increase, K3, knit increase: 7 sts.

Row 6: K3, P1, K3.

Row 7: Knit across.

Row 8: K3, P1, K3.

Rows 9 and 10: Repeat Rows 7 and 8.

Row 11: K2, slip 1, K2 tog, PSSO, K2: 5 sts.

Row 12: K2, P1, K2.

Row 13: K1, slip 1, K2 tog, PSSO, K1: 3 sts.

Row 14: K1, P1, K1.

Row 15: Slip 1, K2 tog, PSSO: one st.

Cut yarn and pull through last st.

Large Leaf (Make 9)

Work same as Small Leaf through Row 6: 7 sts.

Row 7: Knit increase, K5, knit increase: 9 sts.

Row 8: K4, P1, K4.

Row 9: Knit increase, K7, knit increase: 11 sts.

Row 10: K5, P1, K5.

Row 11: Knit across.

Rows 12-16: Repeat Rows 10 and 11 twice, then repeat Row 10 once **more**.

Row 17: K4, slip 1, K2 tog, PSSO, K4: 9 sts.

Row 18: K4, P1, K4.

Row 19: K3, slip 1, K2 tog, PSSO, K3: 7 sts.

Row 20: K3, P1, K3.

Row 21: K2, slip 1, K2 tog, PSSO, K2: 5 sts.

Row 22: K2, P1, K2.

Row 23: K1, slip 1, K2 tog, PSSO, K1: 3 sts.

Row 24: K1, P1, K1.

Row 25: Slip 1, K2 tog, PSSO: one st.

Cut yarn and pull through last st.

Finishing

Center

Sew 3 Large Leaves around bottom of one Dk Pink Rosebud. Sew same Rosebud to Center of Runner.

Using photo as guide for placement, sew 2 Wine Roses, 2 Pink Roses, one Yellow Rose, and one Dk Pink Rose around Center Rosebud.

Sew Large Leaves between Roses around Center. Sew Small Leaves between Large Leaves.

Corner Rosebuds

Wrap a Base around bottom of each remaining Rosebud and sew in place.

Using photo on page 28 as guide for placement, sew Rosebuds to corners, sewing one Small Leaf on each side of Stem.

Rose Clusters

Using photo as guide for placement, sew one Yellow, one Pink, and one Dk Pink Rose and 3 Small Leaves to Runner at each midpoint between Center Rosebud and Corner Rosebuds.

ROUND CACTUS

EASY

Approximate Finished Size: 4" wide x 7" tall (10 cm x 18 cm)

Shopping List

Yarn (Medium Weight) MEDIUM 4

[3.5 ounces, 170 yards (100 grams, 156 meters) per skein]:

- ☐ Green - 1 skein
- ☐ Rust - 1 skein
- ☐ Grey - 1 skein
- ☐ Pink - 1 skein

Knitting Needles

Double pointed, set of 5

- ☐ Size 9 (5.5 mm)

Additional Supplies

- ☐ Split ring marker
- ☐ Yarn needle
- ☐ Poly pellets
- ☐ Polyester fiberfill

Gauge Information

Gauge is not of great importance; your pieces may be a little larger or smaller without changing the overall effect.

Techniques Used

- tbl ***(Fig. 2, page 41)***
- Knit increase ***(Figs. 4a & b, page 41)***
- Knit purl increase ***(Fig. 6, page 42)***
- K2 tog ***(Fig. 8, page 42)***

Cactus

With Green, cast on 24 sts. Divide sts onto 4 double pointed needles; place marker to indicate beginning of rnd ***(see Markers, page 39 and Circular Knitting, page 40)***.

Rnd 1 (Right side)**:** Knit around.

Rnd 2: Knit purl increase around: 48 sts.

Rnds 3-20: (K1 tbl, P1) around.

Cut yarn leaving a long end for sewing.

Thread yarn needle with long end and slip sts from needles onto yarn; draw sts up tightly and secure end.

Stuff Cactus with polyester fiberfill.

Sew cast on edge closed.

Flower

With Pink, cast on 16 sts. Divide sts onto 4 double pointed needles; place marker to indicate beginning of rnd.

Rnd 1 (Right side)**:** (K1, P1) around.

Rnd 2: (P1, K1) around.

Rnds 3-8: Repeat Rnds 1 and 2, 3 times.

Cut yarn leaving a long end for sewing.

Thread yarn needle with long end and slip sts from needles onto yarn; draw sts up tightly and secure end.

Stuff Flower with polyester fiberfill.

Sew cast on edge closed; do **not** cut yarn. Sew Flower to top of Cactus with same end; secure end.

Soil

With Grey, cast on 12 sts. Divide sts onto 4 double pointed needles; place marker to indicate beginning of rnd.

Rnd 1 (Right side)**:** Knit around.

Rnd 2: Purl around.

Rnd 3: K1, knit increase, (K2, knit increase) around to last st, K1: 16 sts.

Rnd 4: Purl around.

Rnd 5: (K1, knit increase) around: 24 sts.

Rnd 6: Purl around.

Rnd 7: (K2, knit increase) around: 32 sts.

Rnd 8: Purl around.

Rnd 9: (K3, knit increase) around: 40 sts.

Rnd 10: Purl around.

Rnd 11: Knit around.

Bind off all sts in **purl**.

Pot

With Rust, cast on 40 sts. Divide sts onto 4 double pointed needles; place marker to indicate beginning of rnd.

Rnd 1 (Right side)**:** Purl around.

Rnds 2-18: Knit around.

Rnd 19: (K8, K2 tog) around: 36 sts.

Rnd 20: Knit around.

Rnd 21: (K7, K2 tog) around: 32 sts.

Rnd 22: (K6, K2 tog) around: 28 sts.

Rnd 23: Knit around.

Rnd 24: (K5, K2 tog) around: 24 sts.

Rnd 25: (K4, K2 tog) around: 20 sts.

Cut yarn leaving a long end for sewing.

Thread yarn needle with long end and slip sts from needles onto yarn; draw sts up tightly and secure end.

Finishing

Sew Cactus to Center of Soil.

Fill Pot halfway full with poly pellets.

Sew Soil to inner edge of Pot, stuffing with polyester fiberfill before closing.

GENERAL INSTRUCTIONS

Abbreviations

ch(s)	chain(s)
cm	centimeters
K	knit
mm	millimeters
P	purl
PSSO	pass slipped stitch over
P2SSO	pass 2 slipped stitches over
Rnd(s)	Round(s)
sc	single crochet(s)
SSK	slip, slip, knit
st(s)	stitch(es)
tbl	through back loop(s)
tog	together
YO	yarn over

KNITTING NEEDLES		
UNITED STATES	ENGLISH U.K.	METRIC (mm)
0	13	2
1	12	2.25
2	11	2.75
3	10	3.25
4	9	3.5
5	8	3.75
6	7	4
7	6	4.5
8	5	5
9	4	5.5
10	3	6
$10^{1}/_{2}$	2	6.5
11	1	8
13	00	9
15	000	10
17	---	12.75
19	---	15
35	---	19
50	---	25

Symbols & Terms

★ — work instructions following ★ as many **more** times as indicated in addition to the first time.

( ) or **[ ]** — work enclosed instructions **as many** times as specified by the number immediately following **or** work all enclosed instructions in the stitch or space indicated **or** contains explanatory remarks.

colon (:) — the number(s) given after a colon at the end of a row or round denote(s) the number of stitches and spaces you should have on that row or round.

KNIT TERMINOLOGY		
UNITED STATES		INTERNATIONAL
gauge	=	tension
bind off	=	cast off
yarn over (YO)	=	yarn forward (yfwd) **or** yarn around needle (yrn)

Gauge

Exact gauge is **essential** for proper size. Before beginning your project, make the sample swatch given in the individual instructions in the yarn and needle specified. After completing the swatch, measure it, counting your stitches and rows carefully. If your swatch is larger or smaller than specified, **make another, changing needle size to get the correct gauge.** Keep trying until you find the size needles that will give you the specified gauge.

Markers

As a convenience to you, we have used markers to help distinguish the beginning of a round. Place markers as instructed. You may use purchased split ring markers or place a length of contrasting color yarn around the stitch. When you reach a marker on each round, move it up.

Yarn Weight Symbol & Names	LACE 0	SUPER FINE 1	FINE 2	LIGHT 3	MEDIUM 4	BULKY 5	SUPER BULKY 6
Type of Yarns in Category	Fingering, size 10 crochet thread	Sock, Fingering, Baby	Sport, Baby	DK, Light Worsted	Worsted, Afghan, Aran	Chunky, Craft, Rug	Bulky, Roving
Knit Gauge Range* in Stockinette St to 4" (10 cm)	33-40** sts	27-32 sts	23-26 sts	21-24 sts	16-20 sts	12-15 sts	6-11 sts
Advised Needle Size Range	000-1	1 to 3	3 to 5	5 to 7	7 to 9	9 to 11	11 and larger

*GUIDELINES ONLY: The chart above reflects the most commonly used gauges and needle sizes for specific yarn categories.

** Lace weight yarns are usually knitted on larger needles to create lacy openwork patterns. Accordingly, a gauge range is difficult to determine. Always follow the gauge stated in your pattern.

●○○○ **BEGINNER**	Projects for first-time knitters using basic knit and purl stitches. Minimal shaping.
●●○○ **EASY**	Projects using basic stitches, repetitive stitch patterns, simple color changes, and simple shaping and finishing.
●●●○ **INTERMEDIATE**	Projects with a variety of stitches, such as basic cables and lace, simple intarsia, double-pointed needles and knitting in the round needle techniques, mid-level shaping and finishing.
●●●● **EXPERIENCED**	Projects using advanced techniques and stitches, such as short rows, fair isle, more intricate intarsia, cables, lace patterns, and numerous color changes.

Circular Knitting
Using Double Pointed Needles

When working too few stitches to use a circular needle, double pointed needles are required. Divide the stitches into fourths and slip one-fourth of the stitches onto each of 4 double pointed needles ***(Fig. 1a)***, forming a square ***(Fig. 1b)*** **or** divide the stitches into thirds and slip one-third of the stitches onto each of 3 double pointed needles ***(Fig. 1c)***, forming a triangle. With the remaining needle, knit across the stitches on the first needle ***(Fig. 1d)***. You will now have an empty needle with which to knit the stitches from the next needle. Work the first stitch of each needle firmly to prevent gaps.

Fig. 1a

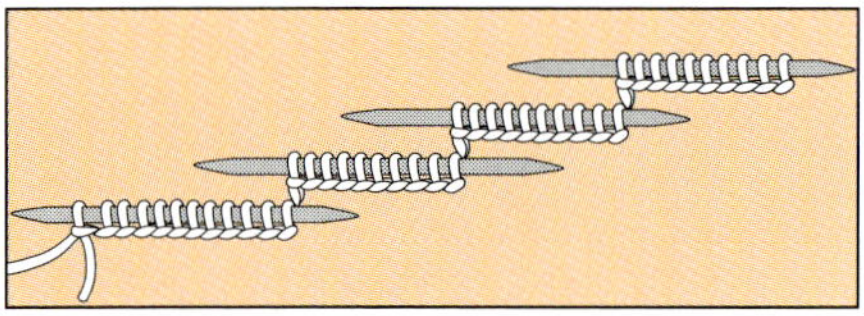

Fig. 1c

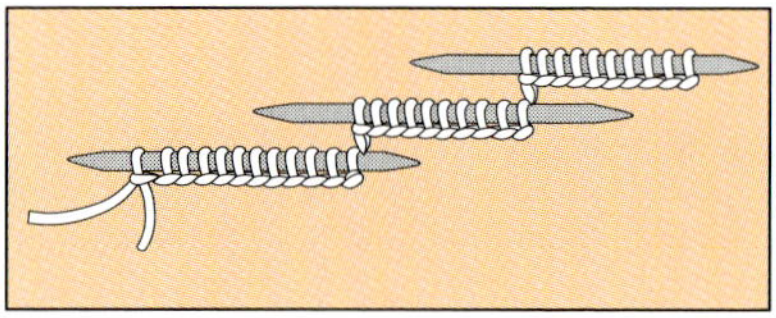

Fig. 1b

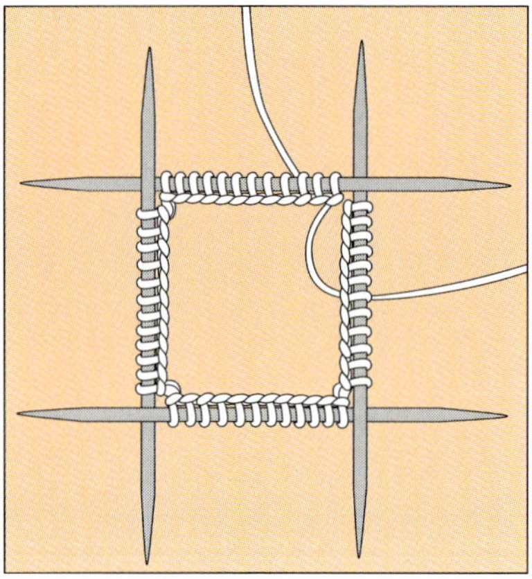

Fig. 1d

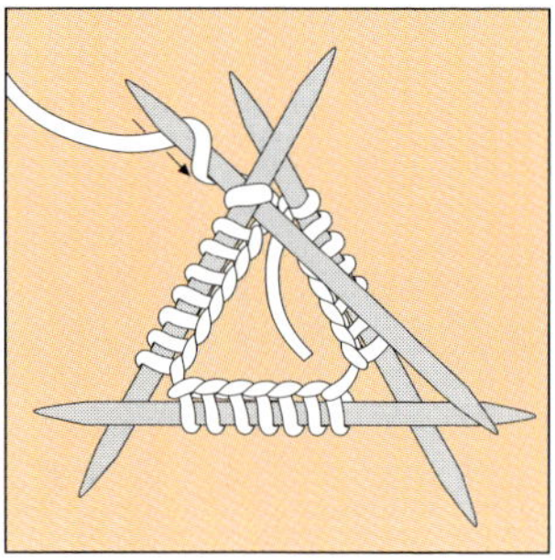

Through Back Loop
(abbreviated tbl)

Insert the right needle into the **back** of next stitch from **front** to **back** *(Fig. 2)*, then **knit** the stitch.

Fig. 2

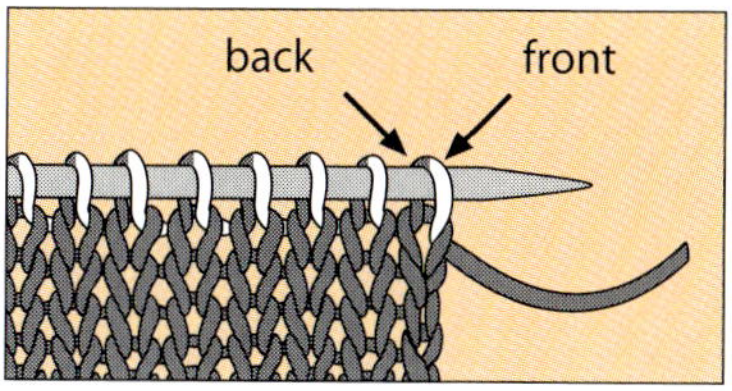

Increases
Adding New Stitches

Insert the right needle into the stitch as if to **knit**, yarn over and pull loop through *(Fig. 3a)*, insert the left needle into the loop just worked from **front** to **back** and slip the loop onto the left needle *(Fig. 3b)*. Repeat for required number of stitches.

Fig. 3a

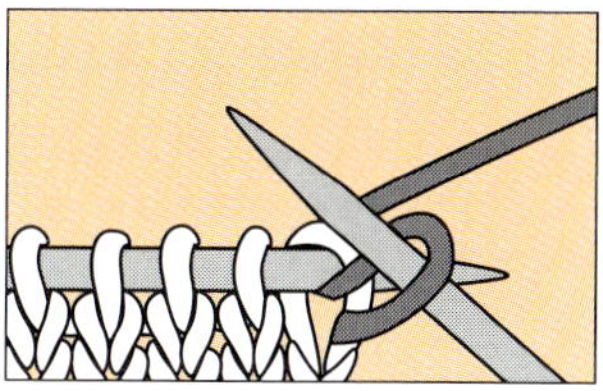

Fig. 3b

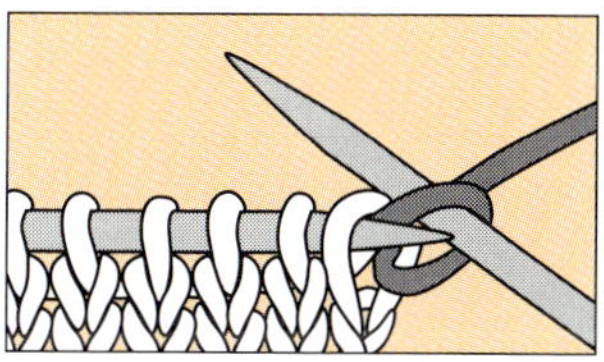

Knit Increase

Knit the next stitch but do **not** slip the old stitch off the left needle *(Fig. 4a)*. Insert the right needle into the **back** loop of the **same** stitch and knit it *(Fig. 4b)*, then slip the old stitch off the left needle.

Fig. 4a

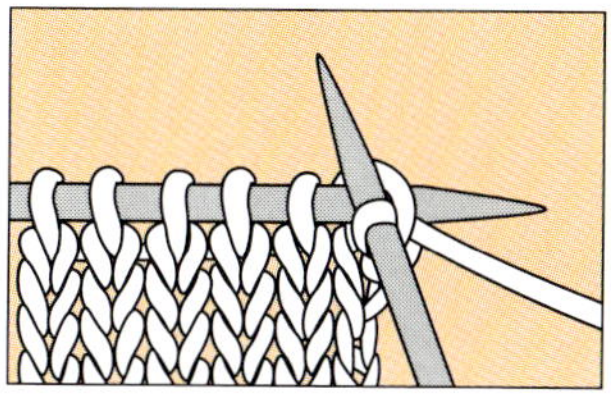

Fig. 4b

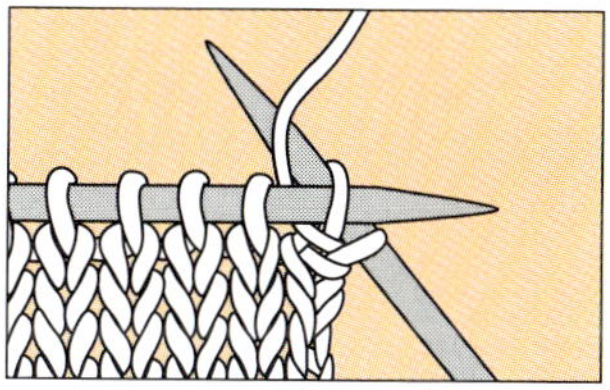

Purl Increase

Purl the next stitch but do **not** slip the old stitch off the left needle. Insert the right needle into the **back** loop of the **same** stitch from **back** to **front** *(Fig. 5)* and purl it. Slip the old stitch off the left needle.

Fig. 5

Knit Purl Increase

Knit the next stitch but do **not** slip the old stitch off the left needle. Bring the yarn to the **front** and purl into the **front** loop of the **same** stitch *(Fig. 6)*, then slip the old stitch off the left needle.

Fig. 6

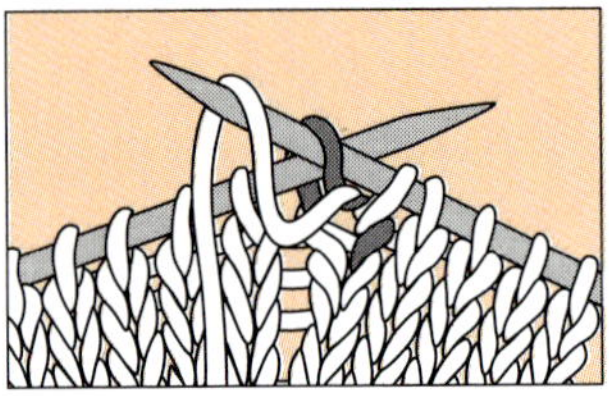

Yarn Over *(abbreviated YO)*

Bring the yarn forward **between** the needles, then back **over** the top of the right hand needle, so that it is now in position to knit the next stitch *(Fig. 7)*.

Fig. 7

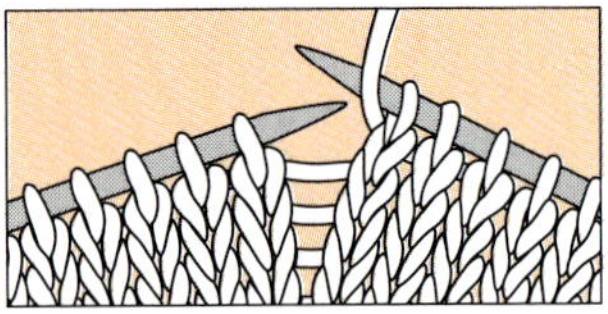

Decreases

Knit 2 Together *(abbreviated K2 tog)*

Insert the right needle into the **front** of the first two stitches on the left needle as if to **knit** *(Fig. 8)*, then **knit** them together as if they were one stitch.

Fig. 8

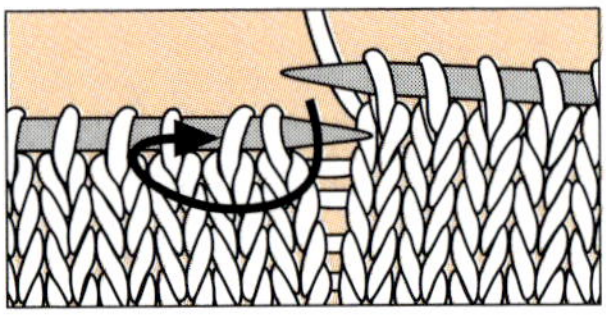

Knit 3 Together

(abbreviated K3 tog)

Insert the right needle into the **front** of the first three stitches on the left needle as if to **knit** ***(Fig. 9)***, then **knit** them together as if they were one stitch.

Fig. 9

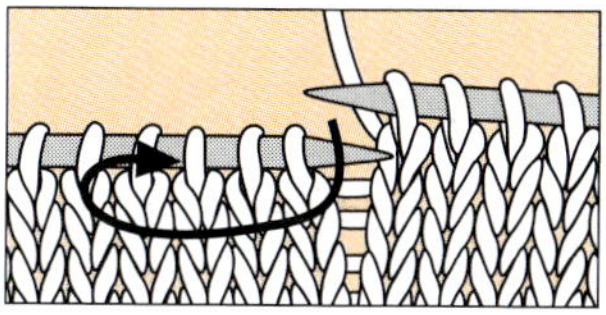

Slip 1, Knit 1, Pass Slipped Stitch Over

(abbreviated slip 1, K1, PSSO)

Slip one stitch as if to **knit** ***(Fig. 10a)***. Knit the next stitch. With the left needle, bring the slipped stitch over the knit stitch ***(Fig. 10b)*** and off the needle.

Fig. 10a

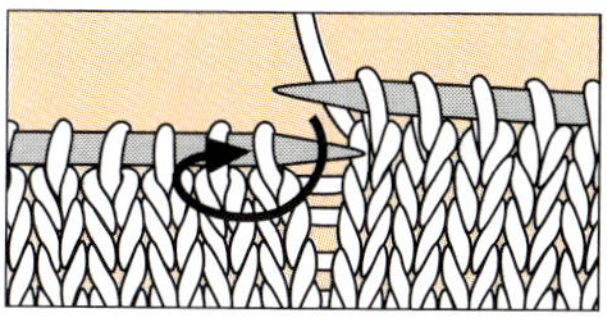

Fig. 10b

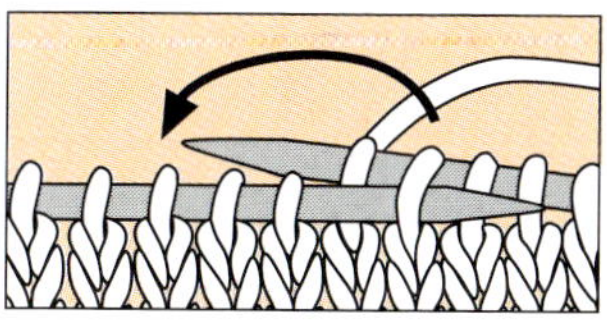

Slip 1, Knit 2 Together, Pass Slipped Stitch Over

(abbreviated slip 1, K2 tog, PSSO)

Slip one stitch as if to **knit** ***(Fig. 10a)***, then knit the next two stitches together ***(Fig. 8, page 42)***. With the left needle, bring the slipped stitch over the stitch just made ***(Fig. 11)*** and off the needle.

Fig. 11

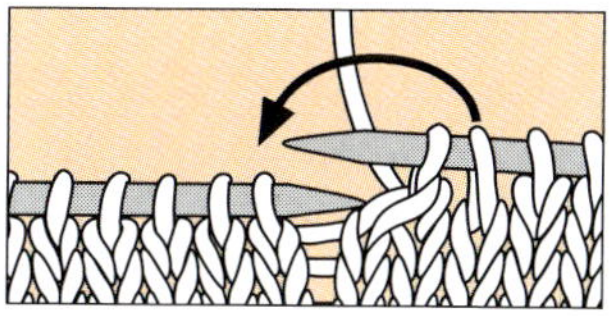

Slip 1, Knit 2, Pass Slipped Stitch Over

(abbreviated slip 1, K2, PSSO)

Slip one stitch as if to **knit** ***(Fig. 10a, page 43)***. Knit the next two stitches. With the left needle, bring the slipped stitch over the two knit stitches ***(Fig. 12)*** and off the needle.

Fig. 12

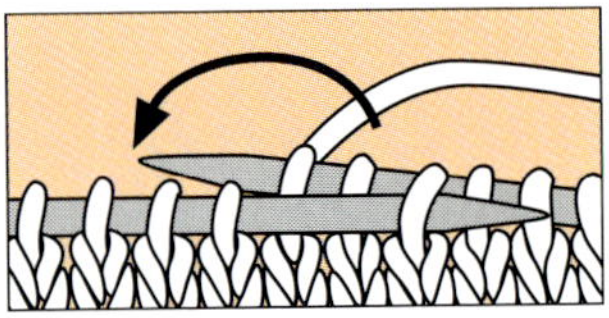

Slip 2 Together, Knit 1, Pass 2 Slipped Stitches Over

(abbreviated slip 2 tog, K1, P2SSO)

Slip next 2 stitches together as if to **knit** ***(Fig. 13a)***. Knit the next stitch. With the left needle, bring the 2 slipped stitches over the stitch just made ***(Fig. 13b)*** and off the needle.

Fig. 13a

Fig. 13b

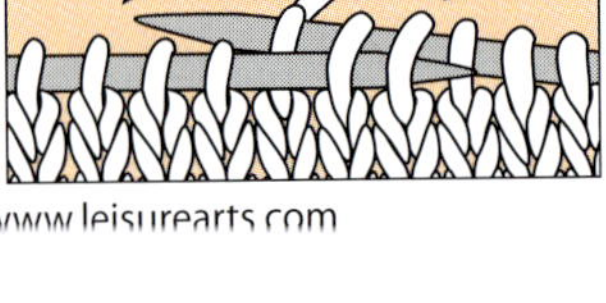

Slip, Slip, Knit

(abbreviated SSK)

Separately slip two stitches as if to **knit** ***(Fig. 14a)***. Insert the **left** needle into the **front** of both slipped stitches ***(Fig. 14b)*** and then **knit** them together as if they were one stitch ***(Fig. 14c)***.

Fig. 14a

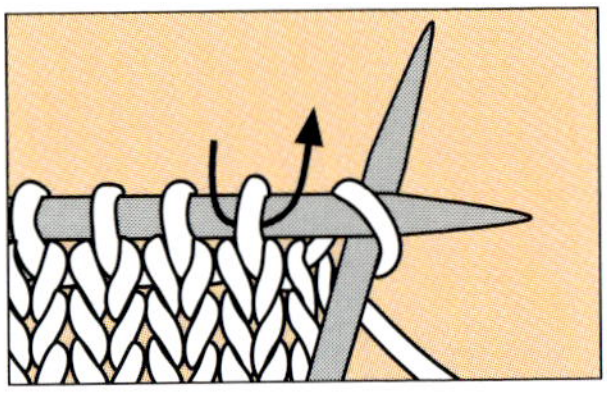

Fig. 14b

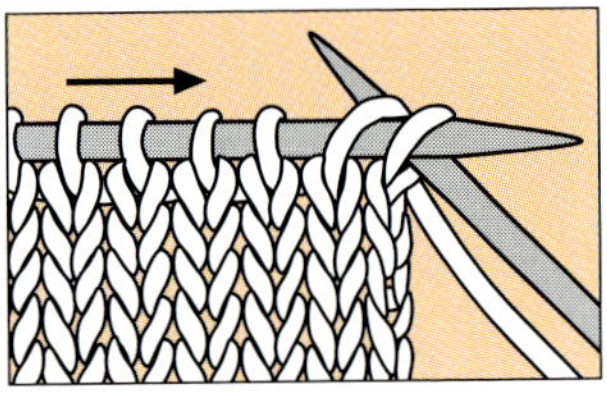

Fig. 14c

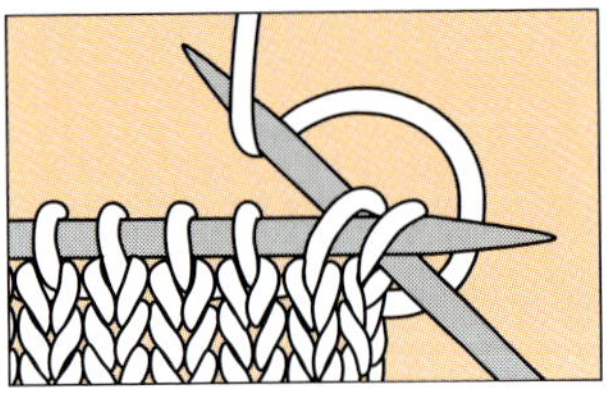

Purl 2 Together

(abbreviated P2 tog)

Insert the right needle into the **front** of the first two stitches on the left needle as if to **purl** *(Fig.15)*, then **purl** them together as if they were one stitch.

Fig. 15

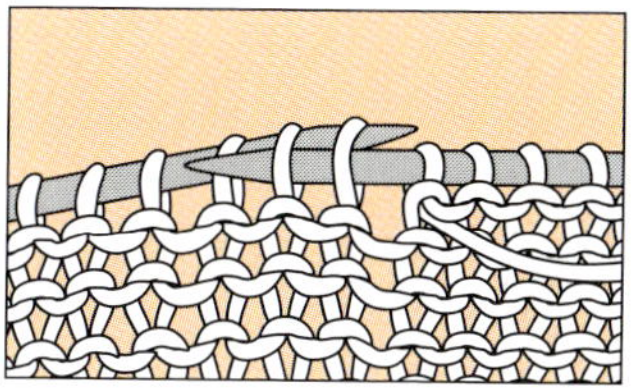

Picking Up Stitches

When instructed to pick up stitches, insert the needle from the **front** to the **back** under two strands at the edge of the worked piece *(Figs. 16a & b)*. Put the yarn around the needle as if to **knit**, then bring the needle with the yarn back through the stitch to the right side, resulting in a stitch on the needle.

Repeat this along the edge, picking up the required number of stitches.

A crochet hook may be helpful to pull yarn through.

Fig. 16a

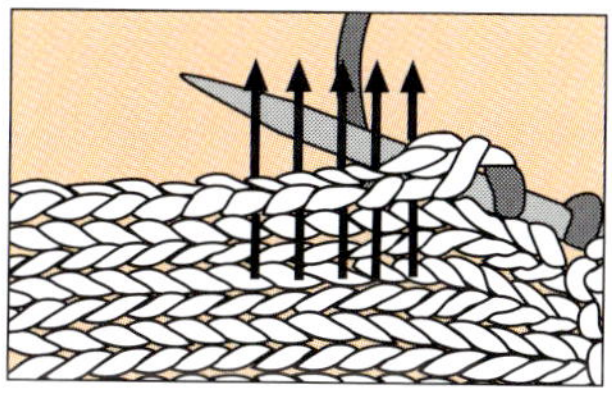

Fig. 16b

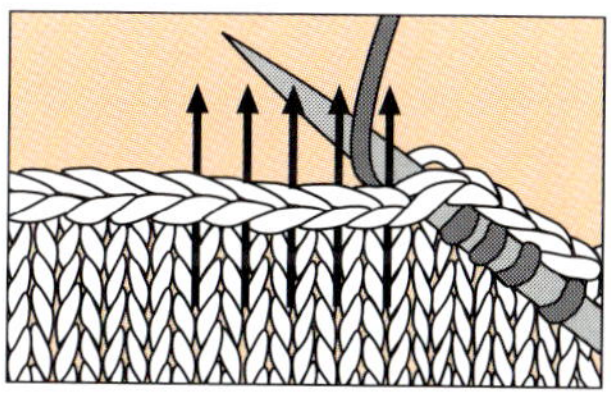

Crochet Stitches

Chain

Bring the yarn **over** hook from back to front, catching the yarn with the hook and turning the hook slightly toward you to keep the yarn from slipping off. Draw the yarn through the loop on the hook ***(Fig. 17)*** **(first chain st made, *abbreviated ch*)**.

Fig. 17

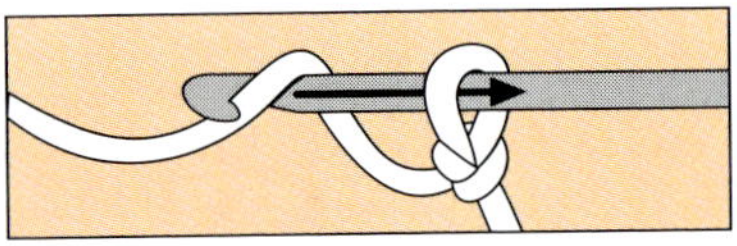

Slip Stitch

To work a slip stitch, insert hook in stitch indicated, YO and draw through stitch and through loop on hook ***(Fig. 19)*** **(slip stitch made, *abbreviated slip st*)**.

Fig. 20

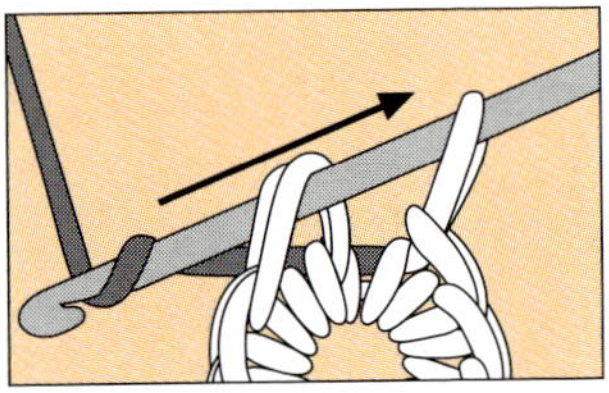

Single Crochet

With slip knot on hook, insert hook in ring, YO and pull up a loop, YO and draw through both loops on hook ***(Fig. 18)*** **(first single crochet made, *abbreviated sc*)**.

Fig. 18

Finish Off

After the last stitch is made, cut the yarn. Bring the loose end through the last loop on your hook and tighten it ***(Fig. 20)***.

Fig. 20

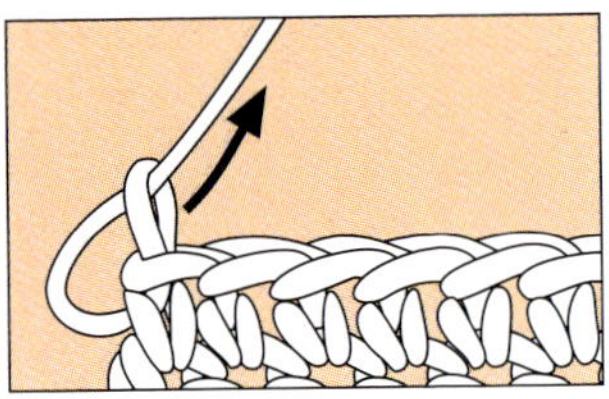

YARN INFORMATION

The items in this book were made using a variety of yarns. Any brand of the specific weight of yarn may be used. It is best to refer to the yardage/meters when determining how many balls or skeins to purchase. Remember, to achieve the same look, it is the weight of yarn that is important, not the brand of yarn.

For your convenience, listed below and on the next page are the specific yarns used to create our photography models. Because yarn manufacturers make frequent changes to their product lines, you may sometimes find it necessary to use a substitute yarn or to search for the discontinued product at alternate suppliers (locally or online).

Cactus Pincushion
Lion Brand® 24/7 Cotton®
Green - #172 Grass
Yellow - #157 Lemon

Coasters
Lion Brand® 24/7 Cotton®
Yellow - #157 Lemon
Brown - #126 Café Au Lait
Gold - #124 Camel

Sachet Bag
Premier® Yarn Cotton Fair®
Cream - #27-02 Cream
Purple - #27-09 Lavender
Green - #27-10 Leaf Green

Mug Cozy
Lion Brand® 24/7 Cotton®
Green - #172 Grass
Yellow - #157 Lemon
Ecru - #098 Ecru

Cactus Garden
Lion Brand® Vanna's Choice®
Grey - #151 Charcoal Grey
Sage - #177 Sage
Dk Green - #172 Kelly Green
Green - #174 Olive
Teal - #176 Peacock
Pink - #112 Raspberry
Lion Brand® Romance®
Off White - #098 Antique Lace

Plant Hanger
Lion Brand® Vanna's Choice®
#098 Fisherman

Bouquet
Premier® Yarn Cotton Fair®
Dk Pink - #27-06 Bright Pink
Pink - #27-05 Baby Pink
Cream - #27-02 Cream
Purple - #27-09 Lavender
Green - #27-10 Leaf Green

Felted Bowl & Vase
Premier® Yarn Boreal®
#1022-10 Cloudberry

Table Runner
Lion Brand® Vanna's Choice®
Taupe - #099 Linen
Lion Brand® 24/7 Cotton®
Dk Pink - #142 Rose
Wine - #144 Magenta
Pink - #101 Pink
Green - #172 Grass
Yellow - #157 Lemon

Round Cactus
Lion Brand® Vanna's Choice®
Green - #172 Kelly Green
Rust - #135 Rust
Grey - #151 Charcoal Grey
Pink - #139 Rose Shocking

MEET ANDI JAVORI

Andi Javori's goal as a designer is to inspire knitters and crocheters to be fearless. "I always recommend experimenting with different yarns and color combinations and to have fun with it," she says. "I like to utilize interesting yarn and color pairings, textured stitches, and other design elements such as fringe, bobbles, or ruffles to add a little sophistication and visual interest."

More about Andi's patterns and kits for fashion accessories can be found on her website, JavoriDesigns.com.

We have made every effort to ensure that these instructions are accurate and complete. We cannot, however, be responsible for human error, typographical mistakes, or variations in individual work.

Production Team: Instructional/ Technical Editor - Sarah J. Green; Senior Graphic Artist - Lora Puls; Graphic Artist - Amy L. Teeter; Photo Stylist - Lori Wenger; and Photographer - Jason Masters.

Made in U.S.A.